The Zones of Paradise

For Margie —

A delight to
share a weekend
of poems with
you!

Akron Series in Poetry

[signature]

Malabar Farm

Sept. 2017

Also by Lynn Powell

Old & New Testaments

Akron Series in Poetry

Elton Glaser, Editor

Barry Seiler, *The Waters of Forgetting*

Raeburn Miller, *The Comma After Love: Selected Poems of Raeburn Miller*

William Greenway, *How the Dead Bury the Dead*

Jon Davis, *Scrimmage of Appetite*

Anita Feng, *Internal Strategies*

Susan Yuzna, *Her Slender Dress*

Raeburn Miller, *The Collected Poems of Raeburn Miller*

Clare Rossini, *Winter Morning with Crow*

Barry Seiler, *Black Leaf*

William Greenway, *Simmer Dim*

Jeanne E. Clark, *Ohio Blue Tips*

Beckian Fritz Goldberg, *Never Be the Horse*

Marlys West, *Notes for a Late-Blooming Martyr*

Dennis Hinrichsen, *Detail from The Garden of Earthly Delights*

Susan Yuzna, *Pale Bird, Spouting Fire*

John Minczeski, *Circle Routes*

Barry Seiler, *Frozen Falls*

Melody Lacina, *Private Hunger*

George Bilgere, *The Good Kiss*

William Greenway, *Ascending Order*

Roger Mitchell, *Delicate Bait*

Lynn Powell, *The Zones of Paradise*

The Zones of Paradise

Lynn Powell

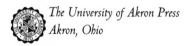

The University of Akron Press
Akron, Ohio

All rights reserved. First Edition 2003.
07 06 05 04 03 5 4 3 2 1

All inquiries and permissions requests should be addressed to the publisher,
The University of Akron Press, Akron, OH 44325–1703

Library of Congress Cataloging-in-Publication Data

LIBRARY OF CONGRESS CATALOGING-IN-PUBLICATION DATA
Powell, Lynn.
   The zones of paradise / Lynn Powell.– 1st ed.
     p.   cm. — (Akron series in poetry)
   ISBN 1-931968-08-x (pbk. : alk. paper)
   I. Title. II. Series.
  PS3566.O83255Z66 2003
  813'.54–DC22

                         2003019702

Manufactured in the United States of America.
The paper used in this publication meets the minimum requirements of American
National Standard for Information Sciences—Permanence of Paper for Printed Library Materials,
ANSI Z39.48–1984. ∞

Cover painting: *Eve*, 1528 (oil on panel) by Lucas Cranach, the Elder (1472-1553). Courtesy of Galleria degli Uffizi, Florence, Italy/Bridgeman Art Library.

For Jane Barnes—
heart to heart

Contents

I

Original Errata   3

You Don't Know What Love Is   4

Etudes, for Unaccompanied Voice   6

Dreading Spring   10

Homage   12

Here & Yonder   14

Late Snowstorm   16

Black Orchids   17

April & Ecclesiastes   19

And the First Shall Be Last   20

II

A Theory of Geography   25

Leeward of Beyond   26

Larder with Christ at Emmaus   29

Swamp Genesis   31

Cold Valentine   32

In Praise of My Daughter's Insolence   33

The Gospel According to 3 A.M.   34

Rendezvous in Low Light   36

Gospel   38

Rescue   39

Habakkuk 2:19   42

Naked Ambition   43

III

Lynn   47

At the *Bosque del Apache* Wildlife Refuge   48

Acceptance Speech   50

Aspiration   52

Varieties of Religious Experience   53

Outside the Garden   55

Garden Passages   56

Snail Mail to the Corinthians   59

Snowscape   61

Verses for *The Madonna of Humility with the Temptation of Eve*   62

Revival   66

Eve at the Louvre   67

I

For in the Zones of Paradise
The Lord alone is burned—

—Emily Dickinson

ORIGINAL ERRATA

He thought He had made himself perfectly clear:
Let there be lust.

But where there's a will, there's a way
to misunderstand, to make tragic
puzzles of shame and fruit
from lovely ambiguities He had always felt.
No wonder He receded
farther than the stars, farther
than the white room of Emily Dickinson.

He'd had such hopes for the garden:
a slow eureka of tongues in understated moonlight,
rosy virtuosities at dawn, even the pink
loneliness at noon the right hand heals.

Thus, He greeted the first tenants
of the flesh, then paused beside the pear.

He wanted to confide a brazen sweetness—
the short, slippery slope
He had made for them
into love.

YOU DON'T KNOW WHAT LOVE IS

You can tell from across the intersection
who's listening to a love song:
windows rolled up, eyes shut to the red light,
heart idling a little too high—like that woman
in the soundproof studio of her Mazda,
swaying, shaking a moan out of her hair, mouthing
reckless stanzas she really needs
for him to know.

Anyone else can see he isn't there, that he left
early by another route and is skirting
this crossroads of Main and Easy Broad—.
A horn startles her, and she
steadies her face, shifts, turns
down the long, thin road toward *tonight*,
that place she'll wear her ache like a small
accessory, an edgy brooch
or silk scarf the color of his eyes.

Well, go on, cast the first laugh, but,
after the crushed orchid of the slow dance
and the duet at the shaky ceremony,
have you ever slipped into a love song
anything but alone?

Haven't you had your own episodes
of Ella, lapses into Janis, Top Hit
spasms of honesty speeding away

from the one you loved?
You've never been willing to say
what you've been willing to sing.

Even last night, sunk
in a soft, late chair, you chose a chanteuse,
and, gazing in the mirror of her burgundy voice,
you believed each *trompe le coeur* she made
with a handful of rhymes and the frank
companionship of a sax.

You wanted to let love have its way
with your words. You wanted to
drown out the bitter
medicine of the moon and jilt
the careful silence, embracing

the naked cry
shameless in another throat.

ETUDES, FOR UNACCOMPANIED VOICE

1

Is it better to be the crocus,
speaking up too soon, putting
a purple foot
in the snow's white mouth,

or to be the mum, mulling
over its maroon, holding out
for the last dark word
on the subject of summer?

2

April, and every apple tree's a diva,
our little orchard smug with Dolly Partons
and the chaste arias of *La Bohème.*
The rest of the season they'll eke out
only a few whole notes for the yellow jackets,

but nobody's a no-show for this brief, white run.
Look at them: bending and bowing,
each one sure the tumult rolling in
from the back row of the horizon is
meant for only her.

3

The frost-tired ground's in the mood for mud.

And maples in strips of curb lawn, redbuds
poised in side yards, dogwoods stalled

between the porch and the open gate—
they're all trying out
their red and pink opinions
after the large, gray, censorious season.

And before green clouds gather in the branches
to drown them out.

4

At first you think a bird's gone
berserk in the dark maple,
that blotch of black against the sprinkled stars.

Nobody around here ever goes out on a limb like that,
this late or this loud.
It's a robin on steroids, a starling
sweet-talking its way into the dreams
of finches and cardinals. . . .

When you find yourself mocking
the mockingbird, stumped by its southern riff,
you know you've lived too long
at the wrong latitude.
What cynic misnamed that bird, anyway—
that earnest DJ of spring?

5

Everything has its say.

Small gray birds chip
at the silence.

Forsythia belts out bright arpeggios.

Even the magnolia, alone
in the dark, corroborates
the moon's white lie.

To all of which the frost
takes cold exception,
in a gloss of asterisks.

6

The body throws itself at the mind's problem,
shrugging out of desire
or despair
with a squall of tears.
And so, for a while, each thought
is solved, relieved of what it knows.

All afternoon, a storm shook
the pear tree at the edge of the orchard.
Now it lingers in the mist,
the way a woman lingers
in the soft
euphoria of the well-wept.

7

Bring in the loudmouth tulip,
the white vow of the lilac,
the iris in its velvet pleasures.
What can fit in a vase, can fit in a voice.

The wind hurries by
in its scarf of birds

and spent petals, undoing both
the naked magnolia and the bold
proposals on top of skinny stems.

Even out of the wind, nothing scarlet stays.
But what would we be without
bright slips of our tongue-tied hearts?
Granite, with a grudge against the weather.

DREADING SPRING

It's easier in winter: the trees
just standing there, skinny
and self-conscious,
like double-entendres divorced
from their better half of meaning.
And the snow falling lightly, finessing
its indifference—till the slow,
mammalian heart shrugs
and curls up in its den.

But what will happen when even the radio
conspires with the weather?
Violins and lilacs reprising their magenta
in every unrequited key?

The Sadhu and the Trappist plan ahead.
They hurl an insult at the possible:
a ring of heavy brass to weigh down want;
some burr or burlap lodged against what's tender.

Should I take their private hint and hide
trinkets of ice to ward off warmth?
Cold words to answer fragrance?

For when the double pane's undone, and between
midnight and me there's
nothing left but lace,

God knows I'll feel again my low
threshold for moonlight,
for the wide, blank sheets of the bed—

where lovers, like poems, are meant to lie,
tongue to tongue.

HOMAGE

Breasts love winter—
they joyride in jalopy bras,
forget themselves in sweatshirts,
mumble their long or short vowels
into layers of wool and fleece.

But just as damned and elect
differently await the reckoning,
some dread, some long for summer—
for summer judges *bosoms*,
boobs, jugs, knockers, tits,

and makes revelation commonplace.
At the marina swimming pool,
a teenager glides past with her new
apparatus, two great spinnakers leading
the languid yacht of her body,

skinny girls wait at the diving board with
their first inklings nudging the spandex,
a prim wife backstrokes in rigid pastel,
divorcées, lax in skimpy black, share
their cigarette-rough laughs,

and a large woman lumbers to the pool's edge
and lowers her flowered suit strategically
into the turquoise, up to a smother
of breasts bobbing like lifeboats
before the *Mayday, Mayday* of her body.

Every tiny assertion, each stiff
insistence, every overzealous nod
is aware of the eyes of men:
powerboaters lounging with
their Budweisers in a cold sweat,

graying skippers glancing up from
Patrick O'Brian over half-moon spectacles,
and twelve-year-old-boys with snorkels and masks
going down for reconnaissance
into the chlorinated underworld.

I bet there's not a cup of milk
together in those two breasts,
sneered my own sixth grade nemesis—
an assessment that defied the basics
of biology but nonetheless

unnerved my adolescence, till I finally
unbuttoned and my first lover murmured
More than a mouthful is wasted
as he sweetly illustrated his
point of view.

Twenty years later in this poolside shade,
my baby agrees: his pink cry
the shape of my stretched nipple,
his eyes and fist and tongue
ravenous and grappling

with what has made him live.

HERE & YONDER

On Jordan's stormy banks I stand,
And cast a wishful eye—

My son's hoping for a swank heaven
engineered on clouds—a Comfort & Joy Inn
where all the good go ever-aftering.
We'll each get our own turquoise room with a view
(assigned on a first-dead, first-served basis),
but we'll gather for banquets of milkshakes and fries,
by fountains filled with root beer, rejoicing
in the holy ban on broccoli,
the everlasting paucity of prunes.

My daughter is pragmatic and fourteen.
Her paradise? I can well imagine what she imagines;
that's why I try to keep her stalled outside the pearly gates.
I know that brand of milk and honey.
I know what waits beyond the first threshold of touch.

An angel's plastered on her shut-tight door:
Johnny Depp, twice her age and naked from the waist up.
Beneath his steady eyes that lock with mine,
I leave my offerings,
Jane Austens and massive Tolstoys,
speed bumps made out of hot-blooded moralists—
though I'll admit that in my time I skimmed
those plots, dog-eared the passions, took
the ardent shortcut.

I'd still know that old heart anywhere—hesitant,
hurried, half Zeno, half Zorro, and bound
for every storm this side of Jordan.

Look: outside my window,
an unpredicted bliss of blue soars
above the autumn baritones.
Yet here I am, stuck inside
one-woman's-worth-of-weather,
making meanings out of molehills, coaxing
tight-lipped verses to eke out what they cannot know—

how far to trust the cobalt happiness
that waits beyond these panicked clouds.

LATE SNOWSTORM

March is a moralist with a highhorse heart,
a spinster with an eager past,
a clairvoyant who reads the orange thought
in each purple mind unhinged by the sun
and blanches.

She despises her own small lapse, and now
all these sudden keepsakes . . .

so she's smashing
her crystal into ten thousand shards
and scorning the crocus with heaps of them—

oh, whatever it takes
to seize up and wreck
the delicate machinery of desire.

BLACK ORCHIDS

Aunt Roxy walked the same sidewalk every
day of the Depression and the hard divorce:
leafy hobnobs of houses, one steeple
needling God, the creek's small talk in culverts
big enough to take the mountain's tirade,
and an avenue of bleeding hearts, forget-me-nots, mums.
She stopped at the iron gate that opened inward.

At that intersection of the quick and the dead,
the bus stopped every half hour, and once,
as she waited with her niece beneath the line of maples
(on strike again and handing out a fiery point of view),
she saw through the wrought bars
a new grave smothered in orchids—
the sod lavished, in that metallic and
ochre time, with a surfeit of purple.
Let's get ourselves a corsage, Roxy said.
That poor woman's finished with flowers.

So they each plucked an orchid from the blanket:
huge, candid, cultivated blooms
to wear all day pinned above their hearts
like outrageous brooches. But as they stepped
on the bus and winked at the driver,
the orchids shriveled in the heat, turned
mythic and dark, charred by the touch of the living.
If that doesn't serve us right, stealing from the dead,

Aunt Roxy laughed, the tender soot falling
down into her lap . . .

                              black petals
now pressed between these pages.

APRIL & ECCLESIASTES

Vanity of vanities, saith the Preacher, . . . all is vanity.

—*Ecclesiastes 1:2*

Windflowers edging their way out of the garden,
violets hinting to the plush grass, bluets
lazing in cloud nines—wherever
you are, you can sink
to your knees in lapis and lavender.

Even the scraggle of woods, rank
with snowmelt and leaf rot,
wades into drifts of sorrel, pools of trout lilies,
while peepers make a ruckus
and, one by one, the iridescents hatch.

It's a swig of Eden, a rendezvous
of promises, the luxuries of lust
before anybody gets hurt—

and only a spoilsport who's been
around too few or too many times would
want to point out the waste it all is coming to:

just beyond hyperboles
of sweet pea, the brassy
glamour of goldenrod,
the cattails' last delirium of seed.

AND THE FIRST SHALL BE LAST

Avon Ladies, gaze on this and weep:
a handsome zealot's on my doorstep, tempting me
with the make-over to die for.
No lush scourge of loofah and mint mud,
no lily-of-the-valley bath salts or baubles
of scented oil can cleanse and heal
like the ointment of belief.

That dirty, little business of the grave is bygones
in the pastel paradise he riffles through,
and everybody's twenty-something, trim, and smiling.
And then my buff believer lifts those dark brown eyes
and judges me. Yes, I have a few faux pas of gray,
and a recent, forty-something aptitude for chins, but still
I'm startled when he condescends, *Ma'am,*
take heart, our Lord makes all things new.
I want to reassure him I look different in another light—
but maybe even that's no longer true.
I tell my heart to harden, before I
backslide through the closing door.

Not a hair of your head shall perish, promised Luke.
And in Torcello, at the gold flash of Gabriel's horn, I saw
lions retort with torsos they once relished,
hands and feet blurt from mouths of wolves,
heads peer from the maws of blissed-out jackals—
the soul salvaging the body from every
junkyard grave and gut.

But I've misplaced my little lot of beauty, not my body.
And so I'd need to lighten as I rise, casting off
the weight of birthday cakes and barbeque, of chevre and champagne,
my face recanting years of smiles that softened it,
my breasts forgetting heavy miracles of milk until
each nipple lifts, pert and pagan.

But could my belly have my babies and deny them, too?
And who would recognize me sleek and sweet and feral,
everything I've learned of love, downsized
to fit on the head of a pin?

Only you, long-lost Adam—.
I can almost see the rendezvous:
in a throng of holy shoo-ins, the two of us just
barely saved, in our smell of clove and sweat,
our tender, savage appetite.
Let God think twice before He gives us back those bodies!

Unless there is a private moon for us in heaven,
a little lake, the bed of a beach, and the endless ransom
of each flawless night—

nights when I was naked, and unashamed,
and I visited you.

II

. . . properly a noun,
eros acts everywhere like a verb.
—Anne Carson

A THEORY OF GEOGRAPHY

It's hard to believe the startled lake
I moved through that first night is not
still waiting for my warmth, the full moon
locked in by the story.
And that little thicket on the Corsican hill,
how could some goat have cropped it down?
Every time I think of it, it's still a nook of shade,
scented with the midday tryst and tears.
Scholars of touch and untouch, cartographers
of poignancy, we pinpoint
each alp, meadow, boulevard, bed
by what the body knew there.

A piazza's thumbtacked above my desk,
and a cottage in a reckless garden, and a fine white
line of land in touch with the sea—
the scrawled graffiti of parting and promise
now turned for good against the wall,
though everywhere the sky's still letting down
its guard, risking the bluest revelation.

Dilettante of all the latitudes, tonight
I pause above an atlas, recalling vistas
from an old frontier, encampments
in the tent of moonlight . . .
then browsing through the hemisphere, I touch
Barbados, Mallorca, the crumpled silk of the Pyrenees,
the wine-stain Paris—my heart another
Magellan of memory and want.

LEEWARD OF BEYOND

1

The lake's gone limp, playing possum.
That's okay with the cormorant, satisfied
on the shoal, drying
its ragged black into a pictograph for *patience.*
No complaints from the heron, peering
through itself to what it wants.

But this large sail sulks, distracted,
all four sides of the wind shrugging.

2

Islands glisten in high-latitude light,
loaves of pink granite, studded with spruce.

And once we get there, we'll have
another generosity of water to contend with—
slow, miraculous hands breaking
in the jagged multitudes.

3

Sweet iced tea and the honeysuckle vespers,
cicadas and mockingbirds, and a hammock slung
beneath the pink flares of mimosa, and the fireflies'
serene S.O.S.—all that landlocked
clutter of kudzu I was born to

I've traded for this Bluescape
with One Immaculate Bird,

one black-and-white cry adrift
on the glacial melt.

4

One insinuation of breath,
and the water bristles.

It's an old argument:
the wind provoking piqued
and frothy backtalk till a squall
strides towards us in its long, gray robe
and makes the high-strung halyard happy.

The boat leans; the sail's obsessed;
the dark waves leap up
and test their silver linings.

5

A scribble of land, a little rationale
for trees, a random act of rock—
that's enough to make
a haven in the wind's hell.

But where did I get this makeshift heart, gimbaled,
with a flair for leanings?
It rights itself in the mirror-twin of calm,
in water so cold, slack nipples
pucker and own up.

6

Now I see what's too subtle in light:
quiet sheets of the borealis
stirred by a far, black breeze.

Soon the horizon will brim with a moon
I'd like, for once, to wish away,
tell it to hold that one, bright thought.

7

Scrape of anchor-rode on the foredeck, and we're gone.
The cove looks blank without a boat,
without a reason for those ripples.

The great lake we left in shambles
is now soothed into blue, blemished
only by mirage—

only by the light bending
over the horizon and lifting up
the green it loves to long for.

LARDER WITH CHRIST AT EMMAUS

Joachim Beuckelaer
ca. 1560–1565, oil on wood

This painter's put his faith in foreground,
loaded it with all the loot of orchard, garden, and the hunt:
deep, wide basketfuls of figs,
cherries, parsnips, plums, cartographies of cabbages,
white knuckles of scallions, the raspberries'
small, huddled, complicated hearts.
Two pheasants hang from a wooden beam,
flanking a cord of songbirds strung through the throat.
And there's a slab from the butcher: a boar's thigh hovering
just above the tender avalanche of harvest,
in darker versions of the perfect white
of turnips and the flowers' crimson froth.
Wine's suggested by the pewter pitchers.
Bread's tucked up on the highest shelf.

It takes a long while for the eye to wander
to the scrap of background—and then *there's*
the Christ, belittled by perspective
and staggering in from a leaden smear of sky.
Eyes and mouth shocked into pools of black,
he's lurching through the archway, his half-
life of a heart panicked
by the recent chastities of cross and grave,
though two companions steady him, fellow travelers
who won't recognize him till his hands rip up
the evening bread. Together, they occupy a space
equal to the brainy cauliflower, or to the stack
of polished, wooden plates.

In later rooms, the Dutch will tell stories
with imported pomegranates, parrots, oysters,
the carnal spectrum of blooms.
Sometimes the reamed-out socket of a skull,
placed among decanter, vase, and lute,
will annotate the pleasure with its nasty
footnote from the future.

But here in this kitchen heaped
with the ordinary, a smudge of spirit
is still stalling at the threshold:
wan fugitive reeling from the infinite,
and starved for the sacrament of hunger,
the ruddy pear incarnate.

SWAMP GENESIS

No Tree of Knowledge fuming fruit
and nobody itchy to eat it,
no spasms of hibiscus and orchid.
Just the apt greenbriar, the Jurassic fans
of palmetto, the pink of the swamp azalea
rooted in rank luxuries of mud.

And nobody bigger than the virgins—
cypresses taking their own sweet, millennial time,
nodding their heads in a cooler atmosphere
while they twist their knees
out of black water.

The ibis and anhinga hunt, innocent
of names thought up for them,
and the cottonmouth spills its greasy ripple
away from our plank path.
We've veered into the wrong Eden
where nothing's more newly minted than alligators
sunk up to their nostrils in sangfroid.

Then, in a flash of slender
neon and negligee-black, two
damselflies land on the leaf in front of us,
and, in a quirk of courtship, one curves
its long, emerald abdomen down and fastens
it onto the other's head—

as if to make a little joke about the human,
to snicker at the mind entangled
in more recent flesh.

COLD VALENTINE

The opposite of human is maple.
The yin to our yang is phlox.

In the shocked ground of February,
small, clitoral bulbs stir but not
because they're plotting out their purple.
Their guile is gene-deep,
an ache for the gold-smeared bee
in everything they are.

No one in the vegetable kingdom needs
this doily and black glitter.
Nobody out there tries
to rhyme with what they want.

That's why I'd like to turn
and live with the rhododendron—
they care not, neither
do they incite their petals
to anything but pink.

IN PRAISE OF MY DAUGHTER'S INSOLENCE

I got my mouth washed out with soap for sass.
I still recall the lick of Dove's white lye
and recollect the awful aftertaste
that counseled me to hedge, to qualify.
George Washington and Jesus mentored boys—
they chopped down trees or spurned a worried mom,
then charmed the world with righteous alibis.
But good girls reaped their own rewards in time:
stymied poems, a stack of counterfeit;
a pliant heart that didn't know its mind;
and once, from Mother's tongue, the name of *slut*.
True, I often did concur with men—
I'd mute their certain words with my soft mouth.
For I could not tell a lie. Nor tell the truth.

THE GOSPEL ACCORDING TO 3 A.M.

I can't tolerate the moon tonight, how it
weighs in, uninvited.
I know the upshot of its soft white logic.

And how am I to answer—
riddled with scripture
but no longer Buddhist or Baptist,
inept at both the lotus and the zealot?

A Methodist would make up her narrow mind
and lie back down in it,
a Calvinist chalk up another chance
to grovel back to grace,
a Holy Roller wrap herself in rattlers
and wear that devil out.

Beneath their far-off prayer wheel, saffron monks
sink down into a low-pitched wail,
a discipline of moan and growl.
I envy them their holy jokes about the self:
the mirrors painted into cloud and cobalt,
the orange, pointed hats with black-fringe veils.

Here, I am witless in the small, frank hour.
Outside my window, magnolias, petal
by lush petal, magnify the ache.

I should be dreaming in the tongues of angels,
I should marshal all the ingenuities of faith—
but I'm stalled once
more before a darkened glass,
letting moonlight render
me just plausible:

devotee of nothing but desire,
and wild again to do God's other will.

RENDEZVOUS IN LOW LIGHT

Can you remember what we would confide
to one another in that snug café
of youth? I can't recall the whispered logic,
the manifestos of the heart, the gossip.
I know that anybody seemed to rhyme
with anybody then: the jazz, the rim
of lime and salt, each table small enough
to quicken all the urgencies of touch.

And I remember how desire was—pure,
without the tinge of insight. Now we pour
our glasses full of cabernet and speak
the dialect of middle age. (We spoke
in kisses then, we spoke in tongues and tried
to answer every prayer our bodies prayed. . . .)
A better judgment keeps this table lodged
between us now—and keeps our memories hedged.

But candlelight's unruly. It reminisces
with streaks of dark left in your hair, kisses
you in places I once did, and wavers.
The café's filling now. Around us, lovers
congregate like species on an ark,
like new recruits in nature's handiwork—
their turn to seek exotica of skin
and find the common denominator of bone.

Outside, Venus poses as a star.
We split the check, then linger at the door:
that galaxy of candlelight behind us
and, just ahead, an eloquence of dusk
pointing out the guiding principles
of ordinary stars. *What could be* pulls
us close——. And then we turn and choose *what is*,
our hearts, like magi, yearning to be wise.

GOSPEL

When a breast is round and hard
as Mary's was so often in the Renaissance,
it aches for a small mouth to relieve it
of a saved-up sweetness.

The baby cries, and the nipple waits,
if it can, for the tongue, or if not,
as a few painters notice, it sprays its lines
of milk into the mouth of air.

Maddened by milksmell, the baby
roots, latches on, works skin to skin
in passionate nursery with the mother—
born glutton for the good, warm news.

RESCUE

My daughter's rosy with a small fever.
I tuck her back in bed, rub her with the eucalyptic Vicks,
and jury-rig some comfort:
a glass of juice, cough drops, a redbud sprig
in her porcelain vase. When she pouts that I won't
read to her all day, I'm ready with the tape player
and a stack of other voices.

She chooses *Julie of the Wolves,*
in which we're introduced gently to the Arctic:
the tundra green, the chill sky doused with gold.
Julie's lost, but it's an early scene, and she's sure
to find her way with so much polar daylight still rewound.
I blow a kiss—I'm off to my desk
by way of the stove and its simmering pots.

Gold floods our staircase window, too.
I look out at purple murmurings in the yard,
at the magnolia stuttering green and the forsythia
brazen and bold as the Pharisee in prayer—
till the teakettle calls me on, humming
under its breath, off-tune with the radio's aria.
Will I weep someday to remember this?

—the splurge of light I love to linger in,
my daughter cozy with an ordinary flu,
the kitchen with its warm remedies,
its thumbtacked portraits of the family

safe and accounted for, the house at ease?
Steam softens my face as I lift a lid
and watch the water turning into broth. . . .

An hour later, I stall at my daughter's door.
It's more than a storm: it's the dark season churned
by the latitude's white violence.
One kayak heaves on the waves, just visible,
then gone from the searchbeam of the story's words.
Julie huddles on the beach and cries for her father,
who's flung his fragile life into that tiny boat.

A parka of seal fur keeps what it can of Julie's warmth
from the cruel kiss of the Arctic.
Sea lashes her with salt.
Wind holds a knife against her cheek.
And her heart—the shards an ice pond shatters
into when a weight misjudges it—that's
what's left of Julie's heart.

My own daughter is not Inuit:
she's dark blonde with freckles and Welsh-blue eyes.
She's lean, taut as a fox. But she's not here.
She's left this spring and gone on ahead,
out into a territory I haven't warned her of.
Alone in that icescape, she's motionless,
her eyes fixed on the black sea and the desolate shore.

I snug up her blanket, stroke her hair,
and gaze at the blossoms I've surrounded her with:
the orderly vines on her papered walls,

her carpet the color of dropped petals,
the rosebuds dotting her homemade gown.
Call me if you need me, I finally whisper,
slipping out of her room to find my way into these words,

the only way I know to save her life.

HABAKKUK 2:19

For dallying with a false god, the bristly
prophets promise the worst Jehovah has to offer:
scattered mountains, whirlwinds
putting their nasty foot down, scabs
on the crown of the head and stink
where sweet should be, fanners who shall fan
all the pleasures out of Babylon, and horses
bringing the swift news of arrows
and a harvest of human fruit.

So, surely, it is not so bad to be cursed with only woe:
Woe unto him that saith to the wood, Awake;
to the dumb stone, Arise, it shall teach!

Though more woe unto her who turns
to the tulip for its red instruction,
who heeds the honey in the honeysuckle,
who lounges in the moon's pale tents.
Yes, and woe beyond woe to the one
who calls down that white and tender fire
to the altar of her bed,
to the altar of her heart—

and who makes, from some strange verse,
some bitter, hasty, discarded draft of God's,
this ink-graven image
she will not take in vain.

NAKED AMBITION

It doesn't take long to master
the technology of underthings:
the backward buckle and stubborn snap,
the braille of hook and eye, small lessons
we learn in the dark, encouraged
by moonlight, mentored by lust.

But the mind, overdressed
for the tender weather, hangs back inside
its own impediments to passion,
still waiting for the license
of someone else's eyes.

And it's a long fumble down through
years of undoing
contrivances of silk—
the black plunge, the pink constraints,
the closest layer of lace—

until some sweet day the mind
is naked as the first draft of Eve.

Until the mind is where the want is.

III

I've plucked my myrrh with my spice,
Eaten my honeycomb with my honey,
Drunk my wine with my milk.

—Song of Songs 5:1

LYNN

Too American to remember the root,
my parents still chose Welsh:
pool at the bottom of a waterfall.

And it's true, a child *is* a river,
gathering the consequences of who-knows-what
old storms high up in the hills

then smashing those heirlooms white
as porcelain against downstream rock.
If rock relents, away

from the gash the surface calms
into a face of sky. Plants lean in,
looking for their own green selves. . . .

Once I longed for a faceted name
I could flash like jewelry. But now
I am falling like rapids

into my one and only vowel.

AT THE *BOSQUE DEL APACHE* WILDLIFE REFUGE

Everybody's moaning this morning on the AM.
I've cranked up the heat and the honky-tonk,
and, alone at last on this Rio Grande backroad,
a twangy tenor's confiding in me, *Tonight*
I'm crossing over to the Broken Promise Land.
It's 5 A.M., and already he's counting down the hours,
but so mournfully you'd think he was another
Moses at a scenic overlook, doomed
to detour far from that lush valley.

Above the mesa, turquoise makes a thin announcement:
dark's closing down its bar, too,
breaking up the slow dance of stars.
And now an achy alto *can't let go.*
She's headed toward that final chorus
where it all comes clear—the whiskey
and the weeping—but just before she gets there,
I find beneath my wheels
the gravel I've been looking for.
I cut the engine and step outside,
my little hothouse of the human
exhaled in the wilderness of cold.

Is this what has to happen to desire?
Must it go the way of manufactured heat
and the great tear-jerked hits of the heart?
I hurry through the question as I hurry
the muddy path between reeds
and coyote-willows, to see the snow geese,
silhouettes on a plush pond.

They float quietly, like orphaned vowels.
Then from one crude call, one hoarse
proposal at the first twinge of light, they crowd
quickly to a caucus of ten thousand, barking
Here! Here! until the red din that
warms their white down
raptures them in a rush of flame and feather—
uproar in which they swerve and cry and wane,
doused by the horizon.

But the scattered sandhill cranes
stay put, thin-legged, ablaze.
I try to be as still as they are, try to wade
my heart deep into the wait.

Then just as I start back out
the way I came,
a slow,
elegant pair
lifts, one thought
at a time, into the trembling silver.

ACCEPTANCE SPEECH

The radio's replaying last night's winners
and the gratitude of the glamorous,
everyone thanking everybody for making everything
so possible, until I want to shush
the faucet, dry my hands, join in right here
at the cluttered podium of the sink, and thank

my mother for teaching me the true meaning of okra,
my children for putting back the growl in hunger,
my husband, *primo uomo* of dinner, for not
begrudging me this starring role—

without all of them, I know this soup
would not be here tonight.

And let me just add that I could not
have made it without the marrow bone, that blood-
brother to the broth, and the tomatoes
who opened up their hearts, and the self-effacing limas,
the blonde sorority of corn, the cayenne
and oregano who dashed in
in the nick of time.

Special thanks, as always, to the salt—
you know who you are—and to the knife,
who revealed the ripe beneath the rind,
the clean truth underneath the dirty peel.

—I hope I've not forgotten anyone—
oh, yes, to the celery and the parsnip,

those bit players only there to swell the scene,
let me just say: sometimes I know exactly how you feel.

But not tonight, not when it's all
coming to something and the heat is on and
I'm basking in another round
of blue applause.

ASPIRATION

Chattanooga, Tennessee

Farther south they call it *hog jowl.*
Up north they call it *salt pork.*
But we called it *streakéd meat*—

the one Elizabethan elegance
in a lexicon of *liberries, chimbleys,*
y'alls, might coulds, and *sherberts.*

On New Year's Day, for luck, my mother would slice it
ten times the thickness of bacon, the salt in one slice
enough to make a mouth shrivel for days.

Far away, others were igniting sauces,
shaping the daily tortilla, or boiling
mussels from the river in coconut milk,

but we were counting on a mess
of black-eyed peas, a fried slab of pig fat,
and the charm of a name, perfected.

VARIETIES OF RELIGIOUS EXPERIENCE

Sydney, Australia

Each morning I improvise a prayer:
at the untuned piano, I pound out
the hymns I know in a minor key, those four songs
marooned in the Baptist hymnal, uneasy
in a crowd confident of Zion.

Let all mortal flesh keep silence I play too
earnestly for this Tuesday bleat of taxis,
hiss of buses, critique of currawongs in the gentrified
gumtrees, corner whir of laudromats wringing
out the weekend's wrongs.

Great-Grandma writes to ask if we have found a church,
and I wonder if this counts: the refuge
of a cool piano in a sun-saturated city.
I sing each verse twice to accentuate its truth,
but for every song I sing, I've disowned dozens.

Down the street at the Solid Rock Center, they're still
Standing on the Promises. Sometimes I pause outside
and hum along with their amplified zeal.
Like Great-Grandma, they know they're heavenbound,
but she hopes to get there first—

she buys just two days' groceries at a time, too frugal
to leave leftovers in the fridge when she goes.
I should be more frugal, less greedy at the market,
less eager to believe we can eat basketfuls of plums,
mandarins, pineapples, pears before rot sets in.

In this week's wicker, a heft of mangoes,
their firm flesh the color of the robe
of the Buddhist monk I nodded to last night
as he set out the temple's trash. In the muted dusk,
I envied him his saffron, his unencumbered head.

His temple, our rented townhouse, and all
the houses in a line from here to there were built on
sandstone chiselled with Wallaby, Emu,
Echidna, Whale—old dreamings lost
to foundations of cement and balconies of wrought iron.

I stand on my balcony with my dripping fruit.
I saw God, my son once told me. *He lives in a field of snow.*
What could you see? *Just snow. And footprints.*
Whose footprints?
The footprints of people looking for God.

OUTSIDE THE GARDEN

Blue Mountains, New South Wales

I walk with my son in the eucalypt bush,
home of the death adder and the funnel web
whose drop of venom can kill a thousand mice.
That's the bad news.

The good news: the snake fangs are short,
and the spider hates the light.
My child has shed his shirt and draped it on his head.
A walking stick in hand, he's a pint-sized Moses

barging up the mountainside, too busy
for eccentricities of flora. I'm straining
to keep an eye on the path in front of him,
edgy as an angel torn between free will

and the doctrines of a fearful heart.
Oh, his skin is so pink against the bonewhite trunks,
against the blue lance of the gum leaves!
And what can I depend on

but the small thump his boots make,
the snake's quick wits and aim to flee,
the great suffering it's born to carry,
but is reluctant to spend.

GARDEN PASSAGES

The grass comes to its green senses:
it forgoes the blue veronica,
swears off the violet.

And so the yard again is of one mind—

except for quiet zodiacs of clover,
subtle stars where the uncertain
still look for luck.

*

Out so early, I can't find
the way to the orchard,

no light but fireflies having
one last-hour fling.

Nothing to do but wait out
the skittish neon—

and know the familiar
always dawns upon the dark.

*

A morning of trim brown birds—

but I was hoping for a flaunt
of orioles, the blue scorch of a bunting,
the grosbeak's blood cravat.

*

I've let the ground forget
all those seasons of tomatoes,
the beans trained for the trellis
and the rows of radish.

And so the garden's
lapsed into phlox, black-
eyed Susan, daisy, *he loves me,*
he loves me not, he loves me——

ten thousand petals of possibility
where there should be
only harvest.

*

Down by the creek,
the prim patch of daffodils
is now a jungle of jewelweed,
muscadine, loosestrife, and the towering
stalks of some dark ferocity
even Adam and Eve
never were able to name.

*

Between the small, hard hopes of the grapevine
and the sweet rot of windfall apples

stands the flagrant mulberry——

and one robin ripping
out the details of its purple heart.

*

Gnaw-marks on the cedar shakes,
yellow jackets dripping from
hideouts in the sill, and now
a hornet's nest growing
like a gorgeous tumor on the eave.

I could bring in poison.
Or I could watch the hungers
taking refuge in what isn't theirs.
And the one that builds with paper,
marbled in each shade of gray.

*

Up in the green monasteries,
cicadas unwind again their mantra,
and every acre stills
to the discipline.

All but the far reach of the cottonwood—
like me, it intuits
a word on the tip of the wind's tongue,
and trembles.

SNAIL MAIL TO THE CORINTHIANS

Smudged with algae and cattail lint, the dark
glass of the pond no longer shows my face.
Gullible summer—misled again
into September's seedy cul-de-sac.

Faithful ants keep moving mountains,
yellow jackets whet their apple-sweetened brass,
and wind chimes, after the dog days' lull,
shiver back into a routine descant.
But I've given up on the garden,
those scrawny plants panting for rain—
the early tenderness that bolted,
the Romas that burned
while I fiddled with wayward words.

There's another huge mistake beneath the lilac:
one spore, bloated on moonlight, imagining
itself as manna.
I heft it like the head of a puffed-up prophet,
to lob it through buckthorn and trumpet-vine,
that no-gardener's-zone between
my deranged lavender and the niceties
the neighbor keeps in line.

So, which corner of the testament have I painted
myself into this time? Which emporium of verse
have I bullied my meaning through?

Overhead, the walnut dangles its intentions,
a surge of sweetmeat over-packed
in enough hard layers to knock
even a leery woman loony.

That's love in a nutshell, I think—
and scribble down another clumsy revelation
from the garbled Greek, another
valentine I only send
in autumn's mistranslation.

SNOWSCAPE

When nothing's left of the green enthusiasm,
no dropped silks of magnolia,
no sweet rumps of plums,
when all the scarlet dénouements
have blown to brown, and desire
has spent itself down to its net worth
of white—

that's when someone ought to tell the hussy
cardinal to give that red a rest, to learn
the cold discretion of camouflage.

Otherwise, the mind still flares—
and cannot drift into the soft amnesia,
the ample nothing else.

VERSES FOR *THE MADONNA OF HUMILITY WITH THE TEMPTATION OF EVE*

Carlo da Camerino
ca. 1400, tempera and gold on wood

1

This museum will be my refuge,
this painting, my chapel—
an easy mile away from Intensive Care.

The lighting's low, and the window's
shaded in with January graphite.
But the eye, like the heart, knows how
to accommodate the dark.

2

Eve's lying at eye level, propped up on an elbow.
And never has abyss been so good to pink,
the void a perfect foil for her foreground flesh.
She fits into the black like a woman
ready to be skewered in a vaudeville act.
You can tell the painter loves her, the way
he's touched her every place he can with paint.

And he's noticed what she's thinking:
holding the pear, as Hamlet did the skull,
while gazing up at someone who's got everything to lose.
Eve's about to make the choice Mary has to live with.
Yet her waves of golden hair suggest
she's thinking of Rapunzel, too,
and ten thousand times ten thousand other happy
and savage endings.

3

What's missing from this picture? Adam.
Though he's implied in Eve's attentive nipples,
in her open-minded stance.

The serpent's wound his body up a barren stake;
he's a scrawny vine blooming
to a small, bald human head—
more phallic than a penis,
more freakish than a porn star's prick.

And he flatters himself, taking credit.
He doesn't notice how her pink outmeasures his,
how, for half-a-dozen hundred years,
she hasn't graced him with a second glance.

4

Strangers in the waiting room, but we all
pray to the same phone propped up
on a vacant wall, petulant idol
in a shrine of sudden answers.
And now the shrill summons
comes for me: at the end of the line,
a nurse saying, *So far, so good*—

my husband's skull cracked open
and the doctor's hand descending into
wet satchels of memory, solved algebras of love,
the deep bituminous lusts and fears.

5

Mary's throne thunders up
from Eve's black cornerstone,

her middle-aged flesh a far cry from
the strawberries and cream of creation.

She's done the best she can with what she has—
a gilt and azure dress large enough to flatter—
but her bare breast seems shaped
from marzipan and affixed
to her clavicle. And her skin is tainted green,
though it's too early for premonitions of Chagall,
or the mossy afterlife.

True, that headdress would give you
one hell of a headache, each quill
of the gaudy, gargantuan crown
topped off by a cameo: the semiprecious faces
of Matthew, Mark, Judas, John. . . .
They're up high, in the glare of a little spotlight.
But I can see how much they weigh on Mary's mind.

6

My husband sleeps on in the sterile light,
a seismograph scribbling out
the quakeline of his shaken heart, and bands
of bloody gauze comforting the fault.

But here the baby turns his perfect head to look
each time I walk into the room.
It's hard to nurse a baby of that age—
the little tug-of-war between the eye and tongue.

And did he also watch
the painter's nodding brush, and the women
slipping shyly in to kiss

his mother's feet, and the men
who came to touch the tender hem of Eve?

He will never take the breast for granted:
he's unlatched but keeping his moist
claim on the roused, thick nipple,
the dark stem of the milkfruit.

7

A zealot in some other century
made a crude point—
he X'd the serpent's grin
and slit Eve's knee and wrist
as if to cut key tendons of the will.

But when he turned to mar
the face and breasts and umber
crux of her legs,
he threw down his blade, and wept.

8

Mother of the bone button
and the tiny teeth of the zipper,
of burnt roasts and spilt perfumes,
of lipstick on the wineglass, Mother
of the warmth beneath the quilt and the gamy scent,
the rowdy baby and the stretchmark,
the stealthy tumor and the neurosurgeon's knife—

Mother who made the bed we love to lie down in—

give us this day our same, sweet flesh,
our bodies that have borne
the brunt of miracles.

REVIVAL

I'd gotten used to the goldenrod rattling
its empty cup, the bony maples, the prostrate
garden, the wind bothering the oak
for one last brown indulgence of leaves.

Now the yard's changed its hair shirt to velveteen,
and dogwoods tire quickly of their legend, tire
of blood-tipped crosses they have to bear, heavier
than the redbud's, old Judas tree redeemed in pink.

There's rejoicing among the violets
when the backslid earth comes home to the green gospel.
I want to lie down and let them lay their hands on me;
I want to take April as my personal savior.

Consider the tulips, washed in the blood,
the forget-me-nots blue-eyeing heaven,
the privet, the briar, the prodigal weed ready
to be born again, and again.

EVE AT THE LOUVRE

Yet your desire shall be for your husband.

—*Genesis* 3:16

There we are, framed in the familiar mug shot:
our bodies bewildered by your mismatched fruit
and the smooth *terra incognita* of my belly.
I'm raising the first, tart, nuptial toast
as our best-man-and-bridesmaid
holds his sneaky peace.

I remember those orchards—every tree but one
striking the same, exact pose. And all the flowers
synchronized along the straight and narrow path.
But there were fragrances
and fervors I remember, too: innuendoes
of jasmine, the silky aims of tulips slipping
out on the breeze . . .
for it's every garden's goal to go to seed,
to let the chickweed mix it up with coreopsis,
to let white pickets smother in the pachysandra's arms.

No master from that old school could pick us from this crowd.
We've lapsed to middle age, backslid from our perfect
bodies-without-a-cause, from that clueless beauty,
all undressed with nowhere to go.

By now we've cried out in every octave of desire,
thrown paring knives and skillets, licked
mango from each other's lips, and let
tomatoes sit on summer's sill and rot.
Our plot has thickened and thinned for so long—.

They want to paint the fallout of The Fall?
Then let them picture us in bed:
up late and reading by our separate lamps,
though lounging underneath a common quilt
and with a shared agenda for the dark—

two practitioners of paradise,
of a bliss even better than the one we blundered through
as God spit out
the sweetest curse in all of Genesis.

ACKNOWLEDGMENTS

I am grateful to the editors of the following magazines where these poems first appeared, some in slightly different versions:

Appalachian Heritage: "At the *Bosque del Apache* Wildlife Refuge";

The Carolina Quarterly: "Garden Passages," "Verses for *The Madonna of Humility with the Temptation of Eve*";

Image: A Journal of Religion and the Arts: "Rendezvous in Low Light" (under the title "Epiphany");

The Bookpress Quarterly: "Gospel";

The Mossy Creek Reader: "Black Orchids," "Varieties of Religious Experience";

Now & Then: "Aspiration";

PMS poemmemoirstory: "Snowscape";

Seneca Review: "Lynn";

The Southern Review: "In Praise of My Daughter's Insolence," "Revival," "Swamp Genesis";

Spirituality & Health: "Rescue";

U. S. 1 Worksheets: "Cold Valentine."

"Gospel" was reprinted in *Spirituality & Health.* "Revival" was reprinted in *Verse Daily.* "Aspiration" was reprinted in *Cornbread Nation 1: The Best of Southern Food Writing,* edited by John Egerton (Chapel Hill, N.C.: University of North Carolina Press, 2002), and in *Home & Away: A University Brings Food to the Table,* edited by Fred Sauceman (Johnson City, Tenn.: East Tennessee State University Press, 2000).

"Acceptance Speech" first appeared in *O Taste and See: Food Poems,* edited by David Garrison and Terry Hermsen (Huron, Ohio: Bottom Dog Press, 2003).

The epigraph to section II is from Anne Carson's *Eros the Bittersweet,* First Dalkey Archive ed. (Normal: Dalkey Archive Press, 1998), 63. The verse from Song of Songs which serves as the epigraph to section III is a translation by Robert Alter from *The Art of Biblical Poetry.*

I am very grateful to Dan Stinebring and our children Anna-Claire and Jesse for their enthusiasm and support, to Susan Grimm for helpful lunches over rough drafts, and to the group of poets who gave me steady companionship and critique during the writing of these poems: Bob Dial, Tom Dukes, Elton Glaser, Steven Haven, Jeanne Hulstine, Kolter Kiess, Michelle Moore, Jana Russ, Christopher White, and the late Ruth Fuquen. Elton Glaser was especially helpful with the completion and editing of this book.

About the Author

Lynn Powell, a native of East Tennessee, lives in Oberlin, Ohio with her husband and two children. Her first book, *Old & New Testaments* (University of Wisconsin Press), won the 1995 Brittingham Prize in Poetry and the 1996 Great Lakes Colleges Association New Writers Award.

About the Book

The Zones of Paradise was designed and typeset by Amy Petersen, with help from Amy Housely. The typeface, Centaur, was designed by Bruce Rogers in 1914. The cover was designed and typeset by Jodi Gabor.

The Zones of Paradise was printed on 60-pound Writers Natural and bound by McNaughton & Gunn of Saline, Michigan.